MISADVENTURES OF FLORIDA MAN & WOMAN

A Comic Odyssey Through the Headlines

Amanada Arelle   Bec Vickers

ISBN: 978-1-942500-80-3
www.BoulevardBooks.org
Boulevard Books
The New Face of Publishing

Misadventures of Florida Man & Woman
A Comic Odyssey through the Headlines

Amanda Arelle   **Bec Vickers**

To Katie,

Conqueror of cancer & reveler of Florida Man shenanigans.

Drunk Florida Man Tries to Use Taco as ID After His Car Catches Fire at Taco Bell

October 10, 2011

Florida Man Tries to Pawn Stolen Jewelry at Store Managed by Woman Whose Home He Just Robbed

November 30, 2011

Florida Man Bitten by Shark, Punched by Monkeys, Bitten by RattleSnake and Struck by Lightening

Florida Man Attacks Mom's Boyfriend with Samurai Sword Over Missing Can of Shrimp

August 21, 2013

Florida Men Flee from Police in a Canoe

January 29, 2014

Florida Man Says Dolphin 'Seduced Him'

February 5, 2014

Florida Man Rescued from Vending Machine

August 22, 2014

Florida Man Stuffs Chainsaw Down His Pants in Shoplifting Case

November 12, 2014

Florida Man Tries Trading Gator for Beer

December 13, 2014

Florida Man Arrested for Urinating on Waitress at Nightclub

January 28, 2015

"Cops: Is That Your Crack Hanging from Your Mouth? Florida Man: Nope"

February 26, 2015

Florida Man Pulls Son's Tooth with His Camaro

April 4, 2015

Florida Man High on Flakka Attacked Officer, said He was God, and had Sex with Tree, Police Say

April 16, 2015

Florida Man Calls 911, Hits on Dispatcher

June 5, 2015

Puppy Shoots Florida Man with a Gun in Self Defense

September 22, 2015

Florida Man Snatches 4 Million Pounds of Citrus without Paying

September 26, 2015

Florida Man in Darth Vader Mask Robs Convenience Store

November 23, 2015

Florida Man Eaten by Alligator While Hiding from Police

December 8, 2015

Florida Man Arrested for Attempting to Break into Jail

December 18, 2015

Florida Man in French Maid Outfit Nabbed During Prostitution Sting

December 18, 2015

Florida Man Crashes Car into Building While Time Travelling
December 20, 2015

Florida Man Arrested for Allegedly Tossing Alligator into Wendy's Drive Thru

February 9, 2016

Florida Man Bursts into Ex's Delivery Room, Fights New Boyfriend while She Gives Birth

Florida Man Drunk Dials 911 for Vodka

June 9, 2016

Florida Man Attacks a Dancing Flamingo at Busch Gardens

August 3, 2016

Judge Bans Florida Man from Ordering Pizza Over Excessive Prank Calling

August 12, 2016

Florida Man Arrested for Shuffleboard Fight at Senior Citizen Center

September 19, 2016

Florida Man Accused of Driving Around Naked with Electronic Device Attached to His Penis

November 3, 2016

Florida Man Breaks into Neighbor's Home to Pet their Cat

December 2, 2016

Florida Man Calls 911 to Taunt the Sheriff After Torching a Police Car

May 17, 2017

Florida Man Calls 911 Allegedly Asks for Officer to Harass Him

May 25, 2017

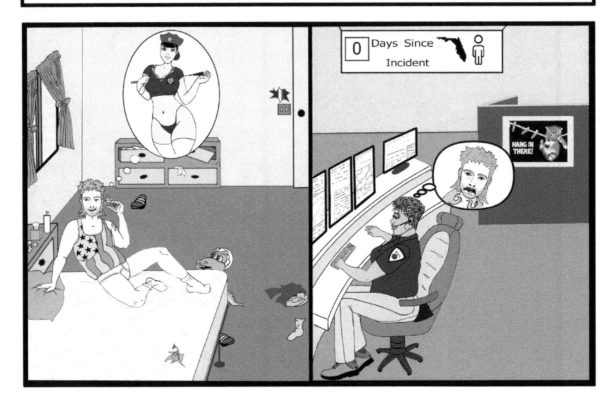

Florida Man Calls 911 Reports Stolen Cocaine

July 19, 2017

Florida Man Sets Scooter on Fire, Tells Deputies He was Mad at It

August 11, 2017

Florida Man Stops to Have Sex During Burglary

August 24, 2017

Florida Man Calls 911 to Request Female Deputies Have Sex with Him

August 27, 2017

Deputies: Nude, Drunk Florida Man Fired Weapons

October 4, 2017

Florida Man Attacks Clerk with Electric Cattle Prod During Robbery

October 13, 2017

Drunk Florida Man Arrested for Driving Lawn Mower on Highway

November 11, 2017

Florida Man High on Meth Climbs onto Stranger's Roof to Howl

November 14, 2017

Florida Man Calls 911 During Police Chase asks for Donald Trump

November 15, 2017

Florida Man Stops During Police Chase to Shoot Up Heroin

November 30, 2017

Florida Man Urinates in Middle of Steak N' Shake

December 11, 2017

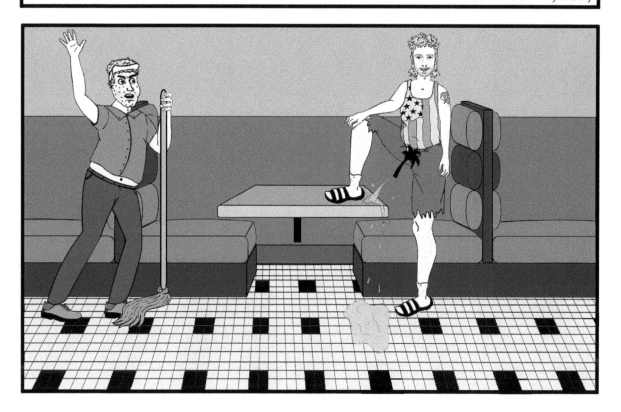

Florida Man Who Marooned Himself on Lake Eola Fountain Says He Took too Much MDMA and Wanted to be with the Swans

December 19, 2017

Florida Man Repeatedly Calls 911 on Restaurant's 'Extremely So Small Clams'

December 26, 2017

Florida Man Says He Punched ATM for Giving Too Much Cash

December 27, 2017

Florida Man Calls 911 to Report Himself Drunk Driving

January 6, 2018

Florida Man Jumps Off Bridge to Escape Drunk, Belligerent Girlfriend

January 10, 2018

Florida Man Rips Urinal from Wall Runs Naked into the Woods

January 11, 2018

Florida Man Calls 911 to Report that His Wife is a Black Widow Spider

January 17, 2018

Florida Man Attacks Girlfriend With Chicken

January 22, 2018

Florida Man Runs Over Himself Outside Strip Club

February 8, 2018

Florida Man Turned Apartment Into Firing Range

February 20, 2018

Florida Man Accused of Stealing Ambulance

March 8, 2018

Florida Men, One Dressed in Bull Onesie, Accused of Trying to Burn Down House with Ragu Sauce

March 21, 2018

Florida Man Kicked Swans as He Practiced Karate

April 26, 2018

Florida Man Asks Troopers if He can Flee Scene of Accident to get Meth

May 1, 2018

Fleeing Florida Man Arrested When His Pants Fall Down

May 17, 2018

Florida Man Caught Masturbating Tells Police He's Captain Kirk from Star Trek

May 31, 2018

Florida Man Told Deputies He was Rolling Joint While Driving

June 1, 2018

Florida Man Dancing on Patrol Car to Save Children from Vampires

June 4, 2018

Cops Found Stolen Zoo Animals Inside this Florida Man's Home

June 5, 2018

Florida Man Calls 911 for Ride to Hooters

June 8, 2018

Florida Man Arrested for Attempted Striptease at Restaurant

August 12, 2018

Florida Man Sings Journey's 'Don't Stop Believin' on Way to Jail

September 12, 2018

Naked Florida Man Starts Fire by Baking Cookies on George Foreman Grill

September 12, 2018

Naked Florida Man Revealed on Video Sneaking into Restaurant and Munching on Ramen

November 12, 2018

Florida Woman Accused of Pulling Knife on Man After Farting Loudly

November 28, 2018

Florida Man Tries to Pay McDonald's Tab with Bag of Weed

December 18, 2018

Florida Man Arrested for Attacking McDonald's Employee Over Not Getting a Straw

January 2, 2019

Florida Man Denies Syringes Found Inside Rectum are His

January 7, 2019

Florida Man Chews up Police Car Seat After Cocaine Arrest

January 11, 2019

Florida Woman Breaks into Police Station Eats Officer's Dinner

January 12, 2019

Florida Man Wanted to Prove Independence to Mom so He Tried to Rob Gas Station

January 22, 2019

Florida Man Prompts Evacuation at Taco Bell After Bringing Grenade He Found While Fishing

January 27, 2019

Florida Man Breaks into Stranger's Garage to Make Coffee

January 30, 2019

Florida Man Flees Police in Handcuffs, Pink Boxers

February 5, 2019

Florida Woman Cradles Baby Alligator in Maternity Photo Shoot

February 9, 2019

Florida Man Arrested After Throwing Burrito at Girlfriend

February 13, 2019

Florida Man Claiming to be 'an Agent of God' Caught Carrying Rattlesnake in Jacksonville Beach February 18, 2019

Florida Man Steals 33000 in Rare Coins Uses them in Change Machines

February 24, 2019

Florida Man Arrested for Throwing a Cookie at Live-in Girlfriend

February 25, 2019

Florida Man Ends Hourslong Police Standoff After Being Offered Pizza

February 28, 2019

Florida Man Steals Toilet Other Items from Home Depot

March 7, 2019

Florida Man Robs Store as Spiderman

March 12, 2019

Florida Man Finds Iguana in His Toilet, Calls 911

March 16, 2019

Nearly Nude Florida Man Rides Bike Backward on Miami Interstate
March 21, 2019

Florida Man Calls 911 Claiming He Paid for Sex, but Got Ripped Off

March 25, 2019

Florida Man Faked Robbery to Get Out of Work, Deputies Say

March 27, 2019

Florida Man Arrested After Saying Heroin was Vitamins

April 4, 2019

Florida Man Buys $8 Million Island then Steals from K-Mart

April 9, 2019

Florida Man Threatens to Destroy People with Turtle Army

April 10, 2019

Florida Man Arrested After Aggressively Eating Handfuls of Pasta

April 12, 2019

Florida Man Arrested After Allegedly Stealing Truck Full of Coffins

April 18, 2019

Florida Man Attacks Mattress After Smoking Meth, Deputies Say
April 26, 2019

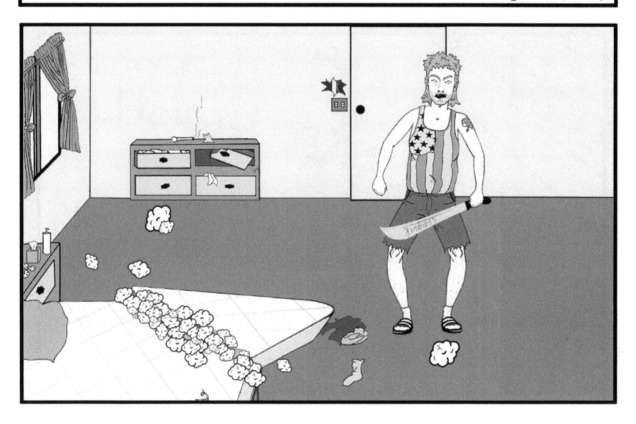

Florida Man wearing Blue Bonnet and Flowery Dress Steals 28 Cans of Baby Formula from Publix

May 2, 2019

Florida Man Shows Deputies His Marijuana Plant gets Arrested

May 2, 2019

Florida Woman Pulls Gator Out of Her Pants During Traffic Stop

May 6, 2019

Florida Man Driving LawnMower Accused of Striking Police Cruiser while Drunk

May 7, 2019

Florida Man Tries to Pawn His Baby

May 8, 2019

Florida Man Stands through Sunroof While Driving on Highway

May 13, 2019

Naked Florida Man Steals from Little League

May 14, 2019

Florida Man Slaps Sleeping Girlfriend with Cheeseburger

May 15, 2019

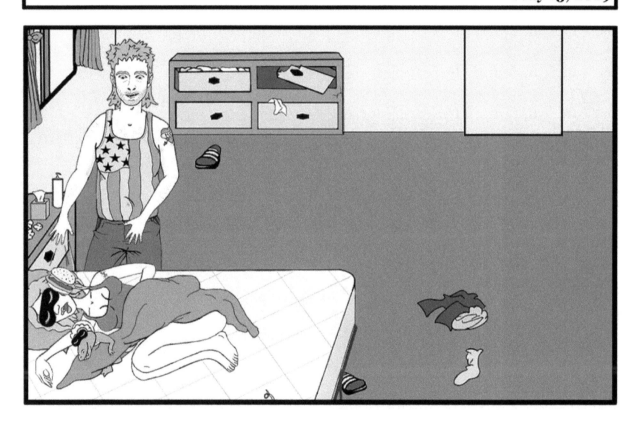

Florida Man Climbs Atop Playground Equipment at Park Tells Kids Where Babies Come From

May 21, 2019

Florida Man Arrested Accused of Hitting Mom on the Head with Corn on the Cob

May 28, 2019

Roommate Wanted Florida Man to Flush Toilet, so He Spat on Her

May 29, 2019

Snake Springs From Toilet Bites Florida Man on the Arm

May 29, 2019

Florida Man Arrested After Driving Off From Deputy, Called 911 to Rub it in

May 30, 2019

Florida Man Arrested After Allegedly Pouring Ketchup on Sleeping Girlfriend

June 5, 2019

Florida Man Found Naked in Chicken Coop After Allegedly Stealing a Car, Killing a Dog, and Chasing a Man with an Ax

June 6, 2019

Florida Man Calls 911 Because "He's Lonely"

June 7, 2019

Florida Man Told Police Cocaine Found on Nose Wasn't His

June 10, 2019

Florida Woman Squeezes Boyfriends Testicles Until they Bleed

June 11, 2019

Florida Man Steals Pool Floats to Have Sex With

June 17, 2019

Florida Man Jumps Canal in Car Dukes of Hazzard Style

June 24, 2019

Florida Man Reportedly Breaks into Restaurant Makes Himself Burger Steals Safe

June 29, 2019

Florida Man 'Tired of Walking' Steals Another Forklift

July 1, 2019

Mixing Poisonous Pufferfish and Cocaine is a Terrible Idea, Florida Man Learns

July 2, 2019

Florida Man arrested for Pelting Girlfriend with McDonald's Sweet and Sour Packets

Florida Man Is Arrested After Befriending Alligator in His Backyard and Feeding It

Florida Man Arrested for Pretending to be a Cop, After Pulling Over a Real Deputy

July 5, 2019

Florida Man Charged with DUI tells Troopers his Dog was Driving

July 6, 2019

Florida Man Arrested After Officers Find Alligator in Front Seat During Traffic Stop

July 8, 2019

Florida Man Tells Deputies He Drank at Stop Signs, Signals only

July 11, 2019

Florida Man Tries to Steal Cop Car with Officer Inside

July 27, 2019

Florida Man Brought Live Gator with Him on a Beer Run

July 30, 2019

Florida Man Uses Umbrella to Fight Beach Goer with a Gun

August 2, 2019

Florida Man Wields Machete, Bat in Fight with Son Over Hedgehog

August 3, 2019

Florida Man Pries Open Alligators Jaws to Rescue Dog

August 4, 2019

Florida Man Opens Front Door, Kinkajou Runs In and Bites Him

August 19, 2019

Florida Man Stuffs Over $50 Worth of Steak in His Pants in Attempted Theft

August 19, 2019

Florida Man Hides More than $1,000 in His Butt

August 28, 2019

Florida Man Cut with Machete in Fight at Bank of America

September 19, 2019

Plants but No Pants, Florida Man Gardens in the Nude

September 20, 2019

Florida Man Throws Bicycle then Other Man from Bridge

September 25, 2019

Florida Man with Machete Starts Car Chase After Stealing Chips

September 26, 2019

Florida Man Attempting to Burglarize Store Gets Stuck on Roof

September 28, 2019

Florida Man Wore Female Underwear Tried Baby Clothes During Break In

October 10, 2019

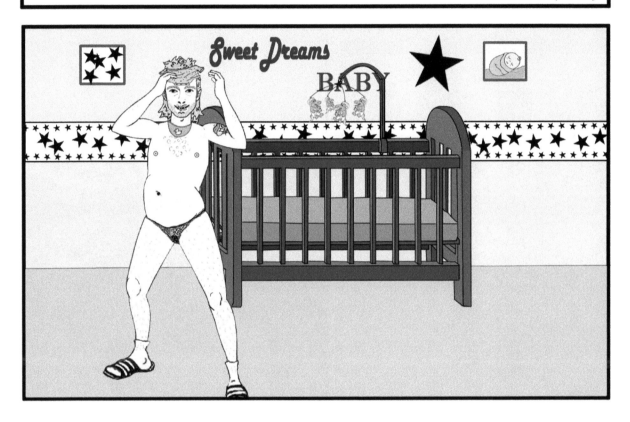

Florida Man Disgusies Himself as a Woman to Rob a Bank, Steals Police Car

October 11, 2019

Florida Man Charged for Sexually Assaulting Stuffed Olaf from Frozen Toy

December 7, 2019

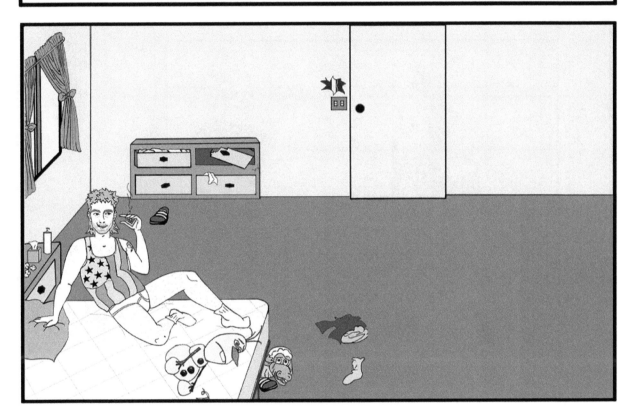

References

Munzenrieder, Kyle. *Drunk Florida Man Tries To Use Taco As ID After His Car Catches Fire At Taco Bell*. Miami New Times, 2011, https://www.miaminewtimes.com/news/drunk-florida-man-tries-to-use-taco-as-id-after-his-car-catches-fire-at-taco-bell-6535056. Accessed 11 Feb 2020.

Munzenrieder, Kyle. *Florida Man Tries To Pawn Stolen Jewelry At Store Managed By Woman Whose Home He Just Robbed*. Miami New Times, 2011, https://www.miaminewtimes.com/news/florida-man-tries-to-pawn-stolen-jewelry-at-store-managed-by-woman-whose-home-he-just-robbed-6523630. Accessed 11 Feb 2020.

Anon. *Florida man accused of calling 911 80 times for 'Kool-Aid, burgers and weed*. Fox News, 2013, https://www.foxnews.com/us/florida-man-accused-of-calling-911-80-times-for-kool-aid-burgers-and-weed. Accessed 11 Feb 2020.

Joseph, Chris. *Florida Man Bitten By Shark, Punched By Monkeys, Bitten By Rattlesnake, And Struck By Lightning*. New Times Broward-Palm Beach, 2013, https://www.browardpalmbeach.com/news/florida-man-bitten-by-shark-punched-by-monkeys-bitten-by-rattlesnake-and-struck-by-lightning-6470152. Accessed 11 Feb 2020.

Munzenrieder, Kyle. *Florida Man Attacks Mom's Boyfriend With Samurai Sword Over Can Of Missing Shrimp*. Miami New Times, 2013, https://www.miaminewtimes.com/news/florida-man-attacks-moms-boyfriend-with-samurai-sword-over-can-of-missing-shrimp-6550992. Accessed 11 Feb 2020.

Mick, Jacki. *Florida Men Flee From Police ... In A Canoe*. Orlando Weekly, 2014, https://www.orlandoweekly.com/Blogs/archives/2014/01/29/florida-men-flee-from-police-in-a-canoe. Accessed 11 Feb 2020.

Mathis, George. *Documentary: Florida Man was 'Seduced by Dolphin*. 2015, https://www.ajc.com/blog/news-to-me/documentary-florida-man-was-seduced-dolphin/CdmDAzgqa8TCmyMfEZBtCN/. Accessed 13 Feb 2020.

Anon, *Florida Man Rescued From Vending Machine*. AJC, 2014, https://www.ajc.com/news/national/florida-man-rescued-from-vending-machine/gCEl3Y90fHtzTaqSMU5J3L/. Accessed 11 Feb 2020.

Riley, Patrick. *Florida Man Stuffs Chainsaw Down His Pants In Shoplifting Case*. Miami Herald, 2014, https://www.miamiherald.com/news/local/news-columns-blogs/deadline-miami/article3798064.html. Accessed 12 Feb 2020.

Marlena Baldacci. *Florida Man Tries Trading Gator For Beer* . CNN, 2020, https://www.cnn.com/2013/12/17/justice/man-tries-to-trade-gator-for-beer/index.html. Accessed 11 Feb 2020.

Anon. *Reptile Shop Owner Hit Employees With Bearded Dragon Lizard*. NBC 6 South Florida, 2015, https://www.nbcmiami.com/news/local/reptile-shop-owner-hit-employees-with-bearded-dragon-lizard-bso/93854/. Accessed 11 Feb 2020.

Online Mail. *Florida Man Arrested For 'Urinating On Waitress' At Key West Club* . Daily Mail, 2015, https://www.dailymail.co.uk/news/article-2929345/Florida-man-arrested-urinating-waitress-popular-Key-West-club.html. Accessed 11 Feb 2020.

Anon. Cops: *Is that your crack hanging from your mouth? Florida man: Nope..*Miami Herald, 2016. https://www.miamiherald.com/news/local/news-columns-blogs/deadline-miami/article62384377.html Accessed 12 Feb. 2020.

Nunez, Alex. *Florida Man Pulls Son's Tooth With His Camaro.* Road And Track, 2015, https://www.roadandtrack.com/car-culture/entertainment/videos/a25442/video-florida-man-pulls-sons-tooth-using-camaro. Accessed 14 Feb 2020.

Anon. *Florida Man High On Flakka Attacked Officer, Said He Was God, Had Sex With Tree, Police Say*. WKMG, 2015, https://www.clickorlando.com/news/2015/04/16/florida-man-high-on-flakka-attacked-officer-said-he-was-god-had-sex-with-tree-police-say/. Accessed 11 Feb 2020.

Anon. *Florida Man Calls 911, Hits On Dispatcher*. Florida Today, 2015, https://www.floridatoday.com/story/news/local/2015/06/05/florida-man-arrested-calls-911-hits-on-dispatcher-big-muscles/28530813/. Accessed 11 Feb 2020.

Scott, Nate. *Puppy Shoots Florida Man With A Gun In Self-Defense.* For The Win, 2015, https://ftw.usatoday.com/2015/09/puppy-shoots-florida-man-with-a-gun-in-self-defense. Accessed 11 Feb 2020.

Holly Yan. *Florida Man Steals 4 Million Pounds Of Citrus*, Officials Say. CNN, 2020, https://www.cnn.com/2015/09/26/us/florida-citrus-theft/index.html. Accessed 11 Feb 2020.

Moye, David. *Florida Man In Darth Vader Mask Robs Convenience Store: Police*. HuffPost, 2015, https://www.huffpost.com/entry/florida-man-in-darth-vader-mask-robs-convenience-store-police_n_5653559de4b0258edb324aed. Accessed 14 Feb 2020.

Tata, Samantha. *Florida Man Eaten By Alligator While Hiding From Deputies.* 2015, https://pix11.com/2015/12/08/florida-man-eaten-by-alligator-while-hiding-from-police/. Accessed 14 Feb 2020.

Anon. *Cops: Florida Man Arrested For Attempting To Break Into Jail*. USA Today, 2018, https://www.usatoday.com/story/news/weird/2015/12/18/cops-florida-man-arrested-attempting-break-into-jail/77561484/. Accessed 11 Feb 2020.

Munzenrieder, Kyle. *Man In French Maid Outfit Nabbed During Prostitution Sting*. Miami New Times, 2015, https://www.miaminewtimes.com/news/man-in-french-maid-outfit-nabbed-during-prostitution-sting-8119801. Accessed 11 Feb 2020.

Frenette, Hana. *'Time Traveler' Crashes Car Into*. Pensacola Business. 2015, https://www.pnj.com/story/news/2015/12/20/car-crashes-through-pensacola-tax-services-business/77667304/. Accessed 14 Feb 2020.

Tan, Avianne. *Florida Man Arrested For Allegedly Tossing Alligator Into Wendy's Drive-Thru Window*. 2016, https://abcnews.go.com/US/florida-man-arrested-allegedly-tossing-alligator-wendys-drive/story?id=36815270. Accessed 12 Feb 2020.

Dennis, Zach. *Florida Man Bursts Into Ex's Delivery Room, Fights Her Boyfriend, Police Say*. AJC, 2016, https://www.ajc.com/news/crime--law/florida-man-bursts-into-delivery-room-fights-her-boyfriend-police-say/pmttIxcdxWxG8rxHfakr3I/. Accessed 14 Feb 2020.

Zorthian, Julia. *Florida Man Arrested for Drunk Dialing 911 When He Wanted Vodka*. Time, 2016. https://time.com/4363426/florida-man-drunk-dial-911-vodka/ Accessed 12 Feb. 2020

Todaro, Chelsea. *81-Year-Old Florida Man Arrested In Shuffleboard Fight*. Palm Beach Post, 2016, https://www.palmbeachpost.com/news/crime--law/year-old-florida-man-arrested-shuffleboard-fight/Sr4TIpiagWFbeTMX2rdywK/. Accessed 13 Feb 2020.

Anon. *Florida Man Arrested For Attacking, Killing Flamingo At Busch Gardens*. USA Today, 2016, https://www.usatoday.com/story/news/nation-now/2016/08/03/florida-man-arrested-attacking-killing-flamingo/87995424/. Accessed 17 Feb 2020.

Anon. *Judge Bans Florida Man From Ordering Pizza Over Excessive Prank Calling*. Fox News, 2016, https://www.foxnews.com/food-drink/judge-bans-florida-man-from-ordering-pizza-over-excessive-prank-calling. Accessed 11 Feb 2020.

Lisi, Brian. *Florida Man Arrested for Driving around Naked with Electronic Device Attached to Penis,* NY Daily News, 2016, www.nydailynews.com/news/crime/florida-man-caught-driving-naked-device-penis-article-1.2856617. Accessed 12 Feb 2020.

Wolf, Colin. *Florida Man Breaks Into Neighbor's Home To Pet Their Cat*. Orlando Weekly, 2017, https://www.orlandoweekly.com/Blogs/archives/2016/12/02/florida-man-breaks-into-neighbors-home-to-pet-thier-cat. Accessed 12 Feb 2020.

Wings, Free. *Florida Man Calls 911 To Taunt The Sheriff After Torching A Police Car*. 97.9 WGRD, 2017, https://wgrd.com/florida-man-calls-911-to-taunt-the-sheriff-after-torching-a-police-car/. Accessed 12 Feb 2020.

Elsesser, Sarah. *Florida Man Calls 911, Allegedly Asks To Be Harassed By An Officer*. Palm Beach Post, 2017, https://www.palmbeachpost.com/news/crime--law/new-florida-man-calls-911-allegedly-asks-harassed-officer/w8WkX691DIzhNalZz2HwQN/. Accessed 14 Feb 2020.

Anon. *Florida Man Calls 911, Reports Stolen Cocaine*. Naples News, 2017, https://www.naplesnews.com/story/news/local/florida/2017/07/19/florida-man-calls-911-reports-stolen-cocaine/492087001/. Accessed 12 Feb 2020.

Elsesser, Sarah. *Florida Man Sets Scooter On Fire, Tells Deputies He Was 'Mad At It'*. Palm Beach Post, 2017, https://www.palmbeachpost.com/news/crime--law/just-man-sets-scooter-fire-tells-deputies-was-mad/0NtB6cEQmEF1DaK4Q69QdL/. Accessed 14 Feb 2020.

DiPentima, Ryan. *Florida Man Stops To Have Sex During Burglary*. Palm Beach Post, 2017, https://www.palmbeachpost.com/news/crime--law/new-florida-man-stops-have-sex-during-burglary/qkqpRpodSuPHLAdkNnBW1L/. Accessed 14 Feb 2020.

Munzenreider, Kyle. *Florida Man Calls 911 To Request Female Deputies Have Sex With Him*. Miami New Times, 2017, https://www.miaminewtimes.com/news/florida-man-calls-911-to-request-female-deputies-have-sex-with-him-6525514. Accessed 14 Feb 2020.

Anon. Deputies: *Nude, Drunk Florida Man Fired Weapons*. Naples News, 2017, https://www.naplesnews.com/story/news/local/florida/2017/10/04/police-nude-drunk-florida-man-fired-weapons/732309001/. Accessed 14 Feb 2020.

Anon. *Florida Man Attacks Clerk With Electric Cattle Prod During Robbery*. Palm Beach Post, 2017, https://www.palmbeachpost.com/news/watch-florida-man-attacks-clerk-with-electric-cattle-prod-during-robbery/a8gThNq6BSHu84wkhWlvHJ/. Accessed 14 Feb 2020.

Anon. *Drunk Florida Man Arrested For Driving Lawn Mower On Highway*. Fox News, 2017, https://www.foxnews.com/us/drunk-florida-man-arrested-for-driving-lawn-mower-on-highway. Accessed 14 Feb 2020.

Nortunen, Sandra. *Florida Man High On Meth Climbs Onto Stranger's Roof To Howl, Police Say*. Palm Beach Post, 2017, https://www.palmbeachpost.com/news/florida-man-high-meth-climbs-onto-stranger-roof-howl-police-say/I01ssv9nPcU55nb91W0irK/. Accessed 14 Feb 2020.

Cadigan, Michael. *Florida Man Calls 911 During Police Chase, Asks For Donald Trump*. ABC Action News, 2017, https://www.abcactionnews.com/news/state/florida-man-calls-911-during-police-chase-asks-for-donald-trump. Accessed 14 Feb 2020.

Anon. *Florida Man Stops During Police Chase To Shoot Up Heroin*. Fox News, 2017, https://www.foxnews.com/us/florida-man-stops-during-police-chase-to-shoot-up-heroin. Accessed 15 Feb 2020.

Stringini, Mary. *Florida Man Urinates In Middle Of Steak 'N Shake In Front Of Dozens Of Customers*. ABC Action News, 2017, https://www.abcactionnews.com/news/region-hillsborough/florida-man-urinates-in-middle-of-steak-n-shake-in-front-of-dozens-of-customers. Accessed 15 Feb 2020.

Wolf, Colin. *Man Who Marooned Himself On Lake Eola Fountain Says He Took Too Much MDMA And Wanted To Be With The Swans*. Orlando Weekly, 2017, https://www.orlandoweekly.com/Blogs/archives/2017/12/19/man-who-marooned-himself-on-lake-eola-fountain-says-he-took-too-much-mdma-and-wanted-to-be-with-the-swans. Accessed 15 Feb 2020.

Peyser, Eve. *Florida Man Repeatedly Calls 911 On Restaurant's 'Extremely So Small' Clams.* Vice, 2017, https://www.vice.com/en_us/article/d343gq/florida-man-repeatedly-calls-911-on-restaurants-extremely-so-small-clams-vgtrn. Accessed 15 Feb 2020.

Anon. *Florida Man Says He Punched ATM For Giving Too Much Cash.* ABC Action News, 2017, https://www.abcactionnews.com/news/state/florida-man-says-he-punched-atm-for-giving-too-much-cash. Accessed 15 Feb 2020.

Anon. *Florida Man Calls 911 To Report...Himself Drunk Driving.* Tampa Bay Times, 2018, https://www.tampabay.com/news/bizarre/Florida-man-calls-911-to-report-himself-drunk-driving_164257768/. Accessed 15 Feb 2020.

O'Neill, Sy, and Eddie Ritz. *Florida Man Jumps Off Bridge To Escape Drunk, Belligerent Girlfriend.* AJC, 2018, https://www.ajc.com/news/national/florida-man-jumps-off-bridge-escape-drunk-belligerent-girlfriend/JHHxtijsgiEK11jkgODG8O/. Accessed 15 Feb 2020.

Michaels, Bill. *Florida Man Rips Urinal From Wall Disappears Naked In Woods.* 2018, https://97x.com/florida-man-rips-urinal-from-wall-disappears-naked-into-the-woods/. Accessed 15 Feb 2020.

Stringini, Mary. *Florida Man Drunkenly Called 911 To Report His Wife Is A 'Black Widow Spider'.* ABC Action News, 2018, https://www.abcactionnews.com/news/region-pinellas/florida-man-drunkenly-called-911-to-report-his-wife-is-a-black-widow-spider. Accessed 15 Feb 2020.

Marr, Madeleine. *Florida Man Attacks Girlfriend With An Unlikely Weapon — His Dinner, Cops Say.* Miami Herald, 2018, https://www.miamiherald.com/news/state/florida/article195958624.html. Accessed 15 Feb 2020.

FHP. *Florida Man Runs Over Himself Outside Strip Club.* Miami Herald, 2018, https://www.miamiherald.com/news/state/florida/article116254448.html. Accessed 17 Feb 2020.

Gilmour, Jared. *Florida Man Turned Apartment Into Shooting Range, Cops Say. Neighbors Woke To A Bang.* Miami Herald, 2018, https://www.miamiherald.com/article201215909.html. Accessed 15 Feb 2020.

Anon. *Florida Man Accused Of Stealing Ambulance.* Fox 13, 2018, https://www.fox13news.com/news/florida-man-accused-of-stealing-ambulance. Accessed 15 Feb 2020.

Anon. *Florida Men, 1 Dressed In Bull Costume, Accused Of Trying To Burn Down House With Ragu Sauce.* 2018, https://myfox8.com/news/florida-men-1-dressed-in-bull-costume-accused-of-trying-to-burn-down-house-with-ragu-sauce/. Accessed 15 Feb 2020.

Gilmour, Jared. *Florida Man Kicked Swans In The Head While Practicing Karate — And Laughed About It, Orlando Police Say.* 2018, https://www.miamiherald.com/news/nation-world/national/article209934014.html. Accessed 15 Feb 2020.

Tziperman Lotan, *Florida Man Asked Trooper To Leave Scene Of Crash So He Could Get More Meth, FHP Says*. 2018, https://www.orlandosentinel.com/news/breaking-news/os-andrew-ecklund-arrested-crash-meth-20180430-story.html. Accessed 15 Feb 2020.

Anon. *Police Arrest Fleeing Florida Man When His Pants Fall Down*. 2018, https://www.nbcmiami.com/news/local/police-arrest-fleeing-florida-man-when-his-pants-fall-down/2009999/. Accessed 15 Feb 2020.

Anon. *Florida Man Caught Masturbating Tells Police He's Captain Kirk From 'Star Trek'*. 2018, https://www.local10.com/news/2018/05/31/florida-man-caught-masturbating-tells-police-hes-captain-kirk-from-star-trek/. Accessed 15 Feb 2020.

Nealeigh, Sara. *There's A Good Reason He Was Driving So Slow, He Told The Cops: He Was Rolling A Joint*. 2018, https://www.miamiherald.com/news/state/florida/article212351584.html. Accessed 15 Feb 2020.

Tribune Media Wire. *Video Shows Florida Man Dancing On Patrol Car To Save Children From Vampires*. 2018, https://fox8.com/news/video-shows-florida-man-dancing-on-patrol-car-to-save-children-from-vampires/. Accessed 15 Feb 2020.

Putterman, Samantha. *Cops Found Stolen Zoo Animals Inside This Florida Man's Home. But More Are Still Missing*. 2018, https://www.bradenton.com/news/state/article212614454.html. Accessed 15 Feb 2020.

Associated Press. *Florida Man Calls 911, Says He Needs A Ride To Hooters*. 2018, https://www.abcactionnews.com/news/state/florida-man-calls-911-says-he-needs-a-ride-to-hooters. Accessed 15 Feb 2020.

D'Angelo, Bob. *Florida Man Arrested For Attempted Striptease At Restaurant*. 2018, https://www.ajc.com/news/florida-man-arrested-for-attempted-striptease-restaurant/dW4yo3CnfYf0LNcywqFsMM/. Accessed 15 Feb 2020

Cohen, Howard. *How Journey's Undying 'Don't Stop Believin'' Figured In A Florida Man's DUI Arrest*. 2018, https://www.miamiherald.com/news/state/florida/article218276035.html. Accessed 15 Feb 2020.

Boggs, Justin. *Naked Florida Man Baking Cookies On George Foreman Grill Responsible For Fire*. 2018, https://www.abcactionnews.com/homepage-showcase/naked-man-baking-cookies-on-george-foreman-grill-responsible-for-fire. Accessed 15 Feb 2020.

Oxenden, McKenna. *Naked Florida Man Revealed On Video Sneaking Into Restaurant And Munching On Ramen*. 2018, https://www.tampabay.com/news/publicsafety/naked-florida-man-revealed-on-video-sneaking-into-restaurant-and-munching-on-ramen-20181112/. Accessed 15 Feb 2020.

Tatham, Chelsea. *Florida Woman Accused Of Pulling Knife On Man After 'Farting Loudly.* 2018, https://www.firstcoastnews.com/article/news/weird/wtflorida/florida-woman-accused-of-pulling-knife-on-man-after-farting-loudly/67-618452313. Accessed 15 Feb 2020.

Anon. *Florida Man Tries To Pay Mcdonald's Tab With Bag Of Weed.* 2018, https://www.reviewjournal.com/news/nation-and-world/florida-man-tries-to-pay-mcdonalds-tab-with-bag-of-weed-1553897/. Accessed 15 Feb 2020.

Leigh, Heather. *Florida Man Arrested For Attacking Mcdonald's Employee Over Not Getting A Straw, Police Say.* 2019, https://www.abcactionnews.com/news/region-pinellas/florida-man-arrested-for-attacking-mcdonalds-employee-over-not-getting-a-straw-police-say. Accessed 18 Feb 2020.

Anon. *Florida Man Denies Syringes Found Inside Rectum Are His.* 2018, https://www.wtxl.com/news/florida-man-denies-syringes-found-inside-rectum-are-his/article_48a3290c-12b9-11e9-800e-dfb4b2e07a8f.html. Accessed 15 Feb 2020.

CNN Wire. *Florida Man Chews Up Police Car Seat After Cocaine Arrest.* 2019, https://wtkr.com/2019/01/11/man-chews-up-police-car-seat-after-cocaine-arrest/. Accessed 15 Feb 2020.

Smith, Jordan. *Florida Woman Breaks Into Police Station, Eats Officer's Dinner, Police Say.* 2019, https://www.ksla.com/2019/01/12/florida-woman-breaks-into-police-station-eats-officers-dinner-police-say/. Accessed 15 Feb 2020.

Smith, Jordan. *Florida Man Wanted To Prove Independence To Mom So He Tried To Rob Gas Station, Police Say.* 2019, https://www.nbc12.com/2019/01/22/florida-man-wanted-prove-independence-mom-so-he-tried-rob-gas-station-police-say/. Accessed 16 Feb 2020.

CNN Wire. *Florida Man Prompts Evacuation At Taco Bell After Bringing Grenade He Found While Fishing.* 2019, https://ktla.com/2019/01/27/florida-man-prompts-evacuation-at-taco-bell-after-bringing-grenade-he-found-while-fishing/. Accessed 16 Feb 2020.

WFTS Webteam. *Florida Man Breaks Into Stranger's Garage, Makes Coffee.* 2019, https://www.abcactionnews.com/news/region-south-pinellas/treasure-island/florida-man-breaks-into-strangers-garage-to-make-coffee. Accessed 16 Feb 2020.

Sweeney, Don. *He Fled Police In Handcuffs And Pink Boxers, Cops Say. It Took Hours To Find Him.* 2019, https://www.miamiherald.com/news/nation-world/national/article198465329.html. Accessed 16 Feb 2020.

Taylor, Langston. *Florida Woman Cradles Baby Alligator In Maternity Photo Shoot.* 2019, https://www.tampabay.com/breaking-news/florida-woman-cradles-baby-alligator-in-maternity-photo-shoot-20190209/. Accessed 16 Feb 2020.

Ewing, Michelle. *Florida Man Arrested After Throwing Burrito At Girlfriend, Deputies Say.* 2019, https://www.actionnewsjax.com/news/trending-now/florida-man-arrested-after-throwing-burrito-at-girlfriend-deputies-say/919363572/?fbclid=IwAR2Qy8hpqYLOVhza5PpdPbcLMNVOyXfMYSLOFtbbRbvFI6izn C5DmkiYl3k. Accessed 16 Feb 2020.

First Coast News. *Florida Man Claiming To Be 'An Agent Of God' Caught Carrying Rattlesnake In Jacksonville Beach*. 2019, https://www.jacksonville.com/news/20190218/florida-man-claiming-to-be-an-agent-of-god-caught-carrying-rattlesnake-in-jacksonville-beach. Accessed 16 Feb 2020.

Leone, Jared. *Florida Man Steals $33,000 In Rare Coins, Uses Them In Change Machines.* 2019, https://www.fox23.com/news/trending-now/florida-man-steals-33000-in-rare-coins-uses-them-in-change-machines/924780861/. Accessed 16 Feb 2020.

Anon. *Florida Man Arrested For Throwing A Cookie At Girlfriend.* 2019, https://www.firstcoastnews.com/article/news/weird/florida-man-arrested-for-throwing-a-cookie-at-girlfriend/77-6f5f5ce2-844c-4ae2-891a-3335433cc450?fbclid=IwAR0dlv2t2BRQnWh2aRM-nBzvFmYCHtQSL-7_p3KIR-PpPFKadwfDGnFUx1I. Accessed 16 Feb 2020.

Makalintal, Bettina. *Florida Man Ends Hourslong Police Standoff After Being Offered Pizza.* 2019, https://www.vice.com/en_us/article/qvyxpv/florida-man-ends-hourslong-police-standoff-after-being-offered-pizza?fbclid=IwAR1AEcvaNmEn8VU8nyKKBrBi9AbJ1yuHbbCvNwK1AtXCVSftD__hiivSH Ok. Accessed 16 Feb 2020.

Anon. Florida *Man Steals Toilet, Other Items From Home Depot*. 2019, https://www.abc-7.com/story/40088647/florida-man-steals-toilet-other-items-from-home-depot. Accessed 16 Feb 2020.

Cutway, Adrienne. *Florida Man In Spider-Man Mask Steals Bottles From Liquor Store, Deputies Say*. 2019, https://www.clickorlando.com/news/2019/03/13/florida-man-in-spider-man-mask-steals-bottles-from-liquor-store-deputies-say/. Accessed 16 Feb 2020.

Anon. *Florida Man Finds Iguana In His Toilet, Calls 911.* 2019, https://www.insideedition.com/florida-man-finds-iguana-his-toilet-calls-911-51469. Accessed 16 Feb 2020.

Tatham, Chelsea. *Nearly Nude Florida Man Rides Bike Backward On Miami Interstate*. 2019, https://www.firstcoastnews.com/article/news/regional/florida/nearly-nude-florida-man-rides-bike-backward-on-miami-interstate/67-a78d16a4-655b-4574-8d0f-bb7864c90b5b?fbclid=IwAR1r-HVwxOmZkerleJIgI25zUnHR1t5vZ1xBtIQ2kvWYGg35bBKeCRP5t8c. Accessed 16 Feb 2020.

Anon. Police: *Florida Man Calls 911 Claiming He Paid For Sex But Got Ripped Off.* 2019, https://www.wtxl.com/news/florida-news/police-florida-man-calls-911-claiming-he-paid-for-sex-but-got-ripped-off. Accessed 16 Feb 2020.

Associated Press. *Florida Man Faked Robbery To Get Out Of Work, Deputies Say.* 2019, https://www.staradvertiser.com/2019/03/27/news/florida-man-faked-robbery-to-get-out-of-work-deputies-say/. Accessed 16 Feb 2020.

Marr, Madeleine. *He Told Cops The Stuff In His Pockets Was Daily Vitamins. It Wasn't Anything Healthy.* 2019, https://www.miamiherald.com/latest-news/article207972329.html. Accessed 16 Feb 2020.

Associated Press. *Florida Man Buys $8 Million Island Then Steals From Kmart.* 2019, https://www.abc15.com/national/police-man-buys-8-million-island-then-steals-from-kmart. Accessed 16 Feb 2020.

Healey, Kelly. *Florida Man Threatens To Destroy People With 'Turtle Army,' Police Say.* 2019, https://www.actionnewsjax.com/news/trending-now/florida-man-threatens-to-destroy-people-with-turtle-army-police-say/938648584/?fbclid=IwAR2PsvANxxeuzopMN5PSyJlMbIN8NZxlrkxk7M2xDSofyM0Dlf8XigO1Qbw. Accessed 16 Feb 2020.

Garger, Kenneth. *Florida Man Arrested After Aggressively Eating Handfuls Of Pasta.* 2019, https://nypost.com/2019/04/12/florida-man-arrested-after-aggressively-eating-handfuls-of-pasta/. Accessed 16 Feb 2020.

Cancian, Dan. *Florida Man Arrested After Allegedly Stealing Truck Full Of Coffins.* 2019, https://www.msn.com/en-us/news/crime/florida-man-arrested-after-allegedly-stealing-truck-full-of-coffins/ar-AABkZV1. Accessed 16 Feb 2020.

Anon. *Florida Man Attacks Mattress After Smoking Meth, Deputies Say.* 2019, https://www.kron4.com/news/national/florida-man-attacks-mattress-after-smoking-meth-deputies-say/. Accessed 16 Feb 2020.

Braun, Michael. *Florida Man Wearing Blue Bonnet and Flowery Dress Allegedly Steals 28 cans of baby formula from Publix.* 2019, https://www.news-press.com/story/news/crime/2019/05/02/florida-man-sought-stealing-baby-formula-publix-while-wearing-abonnet-bedecked-bandit-cape-coral-pub/3651299002/. Accessed 16 Feb 2020.

Officer, Stephanie. *Florida Man Shows Police His Marijuana Plants, Gets Arrested.* 2019, https://www.insideedition.com/florida-man-shows-police-his-marijuana-plants-gets-arrested-52700. Accessed 16 Feb 2020.

Pelican, Garrett. *Florida Woman Pulls Gator Out Of Her Pants During Traffic Stop.* 2019, https://www.news4jax.com/news/2019/05/07/florida-woman-pulls-gator-out-of-her-pants-during-traffic-stop/. Accessed 16 Feb 2020.

Gearty, Robert. *Florida Man Driving Lawnmower Accused Of Striking Police Cruiser While Drunk.* 2019, https://www.foxnews.com/us/florida-man-accused-of-driving-lawn-mower-drunk-after-striking-police-cruiser. Accessed 16 Feb 2020.

Cohen, Howard. *A Florida Man Walks Into A Pawnshop With His Baby. Apparently, This Joke Isn't Funny*. 2019, https://www.miamiherald.com/news/state/florida/article230255619.html. Accessed 16 Feb 2020.

Anon. *Florida Man Stands Through Sunroof While Driving On Highway*. 2019, https://www.nbcmiami.com/news/local/florida-man-stands-through-sunroof-while-driving-on-highway/78843/. Accessed 16 Feb 2020.

Anon. *Naked Florida Man Steals From Little League*. 2019, https://www.nbc-2.com/story/40330461/naked-florida-man-steals-from-little-league. Accessed 16 Feb 2020.

Smith, Jordan. *Florida Man Slaps Sleeping Girlfriend With Cheeseburger, Deputies Say*. 2019, https://www.wtap.com/content/news/Florida-man-slaps-sleeping-girlfriend-with-cheeseburger-deputies-say-509990271.html. Accessed 16 Feb 2020.

Tisch, Chris. *Florida Man Climbs Atop Playground Equipment At Clearwater Park, Tells Kids Where Babies Come From*. 2019, https://www.tampabay.com/news/bizarre/Florida-man-climbs-atop-playground-equipment-at-Clearwater-park-tells-kids-where-babies-come-from_168438881/. Accessed 16 Feb 2020.

Tribune Media Wire. *Florida Man Arrested, Accused Of Hitting Mom On The Head With Corn Cob*. 2019, https://wgntv.com/2019/05/28/florida-man-arrested-accused-of-hitting-mom-on-the-head-with-corn-cob/. Accessed 16 Feb 2020.

Smith, Jordan. *Roommate Wanted Florida Man To Flush Toilet, So He Spat On Her, Deputies Say*. 2019, https://www.ktre.com/2019/05/29/roommate-wanted-florida-man-flush-toilet-so-he-spat-her-deputies-say/. Accessed 16 Feb 2020.

Payne, Ed. *Snake Springs From Toilet, Bites Florida Man On The ... Arm*. 2019, https://www.wkyt.com/content/news/Snake-springs-from-toilet-bites-Florida-man-on-the--arm-510532031.html?fbclid=IwAR3MCyNUJPIWwi_744YdmLH4PV8IXxKEJIZfWzKmiPDnpOZIYqX8F97VOtw. Accessed 16 Feb 2020.

Anon. *Florida Man Arrested After Driving Off From Deputy, Calling 911 To Rub It In*. 2019, https://myfox8.com/news/florida-man-arrested-after-driving-off-from-deputy-calling-911-to-rub-it-in/. Accessed 16 Feb 2020.

Anon. *Florida Man Arrested After Allegedly Pouring Ketchup On Sleeping Girlfriend, Report Says*. 2019, https://www.fox10phoenix.com/news/florida-man-arrested-after-allegedly-pouring-ketchup-on-sleeping-girlfriend-report-says. Accessed 16 Feb 2020.

Bonvillian, Crystal. *Florida Man Pours Salt On Walmart Floor To Get Rid Of Evil Spirits, Deputies Say*. 2019, https://www.actionnewsjax.com/news/trending-now/florida-man-pours-salt-on-walmart-floor-to-get-rid-of-evil-spirits-deputies-say/955474374/?fbclid=IwAR2ayC6Ncoe_PBx87KITa7DcDXYnN-HBAKFnxscAcd0z0n9p7PRLW2Tux1k. Accessed 16 Feb 2020.

Darrah, Nicole. *Florida Man Steals Car, Kills Dog, Chases Man With Ax, Found Naked In Chicken Coop: Police.* 2019, https://www.foxnews.com/us/florida-man-steals-car-kills-dog-chicken-coop. Accessed 16 Feb 2020.

Detman, Gary. *Florida Man Calls 911 To Say He's Lonely.* 2019, https://cbs12.com/news/local/florida-man-calls-911-17-times-to-say-hes-lonely. Accessed 16 Feb 2020.

Via y Rada, Nicole. *Florida Man Told Police Cocaine Found On Nose Wasn't His.* 2019, https://www.nbcmiami.com/news/local/florida-man-told-police-cocaine-found-on-nose-wasnt-his/143868/. Accessed 16 Feb 2020.

Betz, Bradford. *Florida Woman Squeezed Boyfriend's Genitals 'Until They Bled': Cops.* 2019, https://www.foxnews.com/us/florida-woman-squeezed-boyfriends-privates-until-they-bled-cops. Accessed 16 Feb 2020.

Boroff, David. *Florida Man Steals Pool Floats To Have Sex With Them Instead Of Raping Women, He Told Cops.* 2019, https://www.nydailynews.com/news/crime/ny-florida-man-steals-pool-floats-sex-20190617-wpjcb6vmdrh7rhf6tmfoao26c4-story.html. Accessed 16 Feb 2020.

Leone, Jared. *Florida Man Jumps Canal In Car 'Dukes Of Hazzard'-Style.* 2019, https://www.actionnewsjax.com/news/trending-now/florida-man-jumps-canal-in-car-dukes-of-hazzard-style/960565763/?fbclid=IwAR0r9Si3c12gQBLNybHqGIoA3nB_NpvdnatbJcVyrk1iETvMugJMCxXgNPg. Accessed 16 Feb 2020.

Tribune Media. *Florida Man Reportedly Breaks Into Restaurant, Makes Himself Burger, Steals Safe.* 2019, https://fox2now.com/2019/06/29/florida-man-reportedly-breaks-into-restaurant-makes-himself-burger-steals-safe/. Accessed 16 Feb 2020.

Elsesser, Sarah. *Florida Man 'Tired Of Walking' Steals Another Forklift.* 2019, https://www.palmbeachpost.com/news/crime--law/new-florida-man-tired-walking-steals-another-forklift/aWw0XYeqfuUSuSR74e9nTI/. Accessed 16 Feb 2020.

Castrodale, Jelisa. *Mixing Poisonous Pufferfish And Cocaine Is A Terrible Idea, Florida Man Learns.* 2019, https://www.vice.com/en_us/article/ywyjqy/mixing-poisonous-pufferfish-and-cocaine-is-a-terrible-idea-florida-man-learns?fbclid=IwAR33mgNrS0kkcOtCd8lBJFwoxgi-vjcITjgx3ELKBUjOA81QL8t_9FWP6SY. Accessed 16 Feb 2020.

Betz, Bradford. *Florida Man Arrested For Pelting Girlfriend With Mcdonald's Sweet And Sour Packets.* 2019, https://nypost.com/2019/07/02/florida-man-arrested-for-pelting-girlfriend-with-mcdonalds-sweet-and-sour-packets/. Accessed 16 Feb 2020.

Anon. *Florida Man Is Arrested After Befriending Gator In His Backyard And Feeding It.* 2019, https://www.insideedition.com/florida-man-arrested-after-befriending-gator-his-backyard-and-feeding-it-54181https://www.insideedition.com/florida-man-arrested-after-befriending-gator-his-backyard-and-feeding-it-54181. Accessed 16 Feb 2020.

Smalls II, C. Isaiah. *Florida Man Arrested For Pretending To Be A Cop After Pulling Over Real Deputy.* 2019, https://www.miamiherald.com/news/state/florida/article232329097.html. Accessed 16 Feb 2020.

Cohen, Howard. *A Lot Of Things Get Blamed On The Dog. But This Was A New One.* 2019, https://www.miamiherald.com/news/state/florida/article214423419.html. Accessed 17 Feb 2020.

Fiallo, Josh. *Florida Man Arrested After Officers Find Live Alligator In Front Seat During Traffic Stop.* 2019, https://www.tampabay.com/florida/2019/07/08/florida-man-arrested-after-officers-find-live-alligator-in-front-seat-during-traffic-stop/. Accessed 17 Feb 2020.

Anon. *Florida Man Tells Deputies He Drank At Stop Signs, Signals Only.* 2019, https://www.fox7austin.com/news/florida-man-tells-deputies-he-drank-at-stop-signs-signals-only. Accessed 17 Feb 2020.

Anon. *FL Man Tries To Steal Police Car With Officer In It.* 2019, https://www.policemag.com/359698/fl-man-tries-to-steal-police-car-with-officer-in-it. Accessed 17 Feb 2020.

Associated Press. *Florida Man Makes Beer Run With Gator In Hand.* 2019, https://www.abcactionnews.com/news/florida-man-makes-beer-run-with-gator-in-hand. Accessed 17 Feb 2020.

Elsesser, Sarah. *Florida Man Uses Umbrella To Fight Beachgoer With A Gun.* 2019, https://www.palmbeachpost.com/news/watch-florida-man-uses-umbrella-fight-beachgoer-with-gun/ERYLX81cXX5et81eK9l7nJ/. Accessed 17 Feb 2020.

Theisen, Tiffini. *Florida Man Wields Machete, Bat In Fight With Son Over Hedgehog*: Report. 2019, https://www.orlandosentinel.com/features/gone-viral/os-dad-son-hedgehog-fight-20170803-story.html. Accessed 17 Feb 2020.

Leone, Jared. *Florida Man Pries Open Alligator's Jaws To Rescue Dog.* 2019, https://www.actionnewsjax.com/news/trending-now/florida-man-pries-open-alligators-jaws-to-rescue-dog/972509430/?fbclid=IwAR2VjnToDFZefn0isFwWhlJYunAaD57CQgkGUDx4cdDB6vtl8N2tu_4m01o. Accessed 17 Feb 2020.

Healey, Kelly. *Florida Man Opens Front Door; Kinkajou Runs In, Bites Him.* 2019, https://www.actionnewsjax.com/news/trending-now/florida-man-opens-front-door-kinkajouruns-in-bites-him-1/977358424/?fbclid=IwAR0W6J-qaY8hTblTy1Txpz4zVbKrn9IZjE6SFVvPCPHxfzRBsl0NU2ZcEnE. Accessed 17 Feb 2020.

Anon. *Florida Man Stuffs Over $50 Worth Of Steak In His Pants In Attempted Theft*, Deputies Say. 2019, https://www.actionnewsjax.com/news/local/florida-man-stuffs-over-50-worth-of-steak-in-his-pants-in-attempted-theft-deputies-say/976326833/?fbclid=IwAR1KqsJVRKrvVcyoj7JV-8y5hXn9fCs1ZoDHpq11Yw5xNj1ikYRRjpr1wAA. Accessed 17 Feb 2020.

Teproff, Carli. *Florida Man Hides More Than $1,000 In Cash In His Buttocks*, Cops Say. It Doesn't Work.. 2019, https://www.miamiherald.com/news/state/article169902997.html. Accessed 17 Feb 2020.

Todaro, Chelsea. *Florida Man Cut With Machete In Fight At Bank Of America*. 2019, https://www.palmbeachpost.com/news/crime--law/new-florida-man-cut-with-machete-fight-bank-america/mfZO8cMWZW5XYz8zcA4GWI/. Accessed 17 Feb 2020.

Anon. *Plants, But No Pants: Florida Man Gardens In The Nude*. 2019, https://www.nbcmiami.com/news/local/plants-but-no-pants-florida-man-gardens-in-the-nude/152465/. Accessed 17 Feb 2020.

Nortunen, Sandra. *Florida Man With Machete Starts Car Chase After Stealing Chips*. 2019, https://www.palmbeachpost.com/article/20170926/NEWS/812020024. Accessed 17 Feb 2020.

WESH Staff. *Florida Man Attempting To Burglarize Store Gets Stuck On Roof*. 2019, https://www.wsav.com/crime-safety/florida-man-attempting-to-burglarize-store-gets-stuck-on-roof/. Accessed 17 Feb 2020.

Smith, Jordan. *Florida Man Wore Female Underwear, Tried On Baby Clothes During Break-In, Deputies Say*. 2019, https://www.wflx.com/2019/10/10/florida-man-wore-female-underwear-tried-baby-clothes-during-break-in-deputies-say/. Accessed 17 Feb 2020.

Georgiou, Aristos. *Florida Man Disguises Himself As A Woman To Rob A Bank, Steals Police Car*. 2019, https://www.newsweek.com/man-woman-rob-bank-steals-police-car-1464572https://www.newsweek.com/man-woman-rob-bank-steals-police-car-1464572. Accessed 17 Feb 2020.

O'Brien, Rachel, and Paula Froelich. *Florida Man Charged For Sexually Assaulting Stuffed Olaf From 'Frozen' Toy*. 2019, https://nypost.com/2019/12/07/florida-man-charged-for-sexually-assaulting-stuffed-olaf-from-frozen-toy/. Accessed 17 Feb 2020.

Seiger, Theresa. *Florida Man Accused Of Handing Out Marijuana To Passersby 'Because It Was Christmas'*. 2019, https://www.actionnewsjax.com/news/trending/florida-man-accused-handing-out-marijuana-passersby-because-it-was-christmas/22VOOFIAPVFXPGLFDZ7RJMN56I/?_website=cmg-tv-10050. Accessed 17 Feb 2020.

CPSIA information can be obtained
at www.ICGtesting.com
Printed in the USA
LVHW061252260422
717276LV00016B/204